BANGKOK
THE CITY AT A GLANC

G000139334

Mandarin Oriental
Superlative service and silky flo
made this Bangkok institution a
hotel for royalty and visiting VIP
See p016

Assumption Cathedral
Bangkok's Catholic cathedral was completed
in 1821 to serve the city's French community,
and was rebuilt in the Romanesque style in
1909. Its red-and-white brick façade stands
out among the modern towers on the river.
23 Soi Oriental, Thanon Charoen Krung

Jewelry Trade Center
Completed in 1996, this 220m high-rise,
designed by Urban Architects & Associates,
is the hub of Bangkok's booming gem trade.
The Silom Galleria in the lower plaza is a
retail space for art, antiques and jewellery.
919/1 Thanon Silom, T 02 630 0944

State Tower
With its dome, curved terraces and classical
motifs, this overblown building by Rangsan
Architecture was almost crippled by the 1997
Asian financial crisis but since its opening in
2001 it has become an exclusive destination
and now attracts the city's beau monde.
1055 Thanon Silom

Chao Phraya River
Choppy and clogged, this snake-like stretch
of water swells with tugs, ferries, pleasure
cruisers, river taxis and local fishermen.

Shangri-La Hotel
The largest of the city's plush hotels opened
in 1986 and seduces its guests into staying
well and truly put with five restaurants, a
luxurious spa and tropical riverfront gardens.
See p020

INTRODUCTION
THE CHANGING FACE OF THE URBAN SCENE

There's long been a media-fed familiarity to Bangkok, a coruscant whirl that takes in floating fruit markets, street vendors' sizzling hotplates and the Buddhist temple stupas overlooking Patpong's fake labels and full-on floorshows. These days, though, the city also boasts shiny megamalls and a futuristic public transport system, the SkyTrain, alongside its water taxis crammed with office workers. It's a mix of new money and no money – luxury condos sharing the same area code as corrugated-iron slums.

Today's Bangkok smacks of sophistication – the Calatrava-style Rama VIII Bridge over the river, the planting of millions of trees and auto-flush urinals at Chatuchak Weekend Market, while even the tuk-tuks now run on liquid propane. Government-backed schemes to promote the creative industries have transformed the city into a shoppers' paradise, while the Bangkok Arts and Culture Centre (939 Thanon Rama I, T 02 214 6630) and the TCDC (see p036) have opened up new avenues for the ambitious.

You can still do old-school Bangkok, if you like – living out Graham Greene sub-plots, ambling through riverside alleys, being magicked back in time on a canal cruise, fixating on the scorpions being sold live in the pet market and kicking back in the five-star bars, trying to pick out the true *hiso* (high society) from the mere Bangkok bling. It's your call, and it's the frisson produced by this choice that makes Bangkok the beguiling temptress she is.

ESSENTIAL INFO

FACTS, FIGURES AND USEFUL ADDRESSES

TOURIST OFFICE
Tourism Authority of Thailand
1600 Thanon Phetchaburi
T 02 250 5500
tourismthailand.org

TRANSPORT
Car hire
Budget
T 02 203 9222
BTS SkyTrain
T 02 617 7340
www.bts.co.th
MRT metro
T 02 624 5200
www.bangkokmetro.co.th
The SkyTrain and metro run 6am-midnight
Taxis
Siam Taxi
T 1661
Taxis can be hailed on the street and are safer and often cheaper than tuk-tuks

EMERGENCY SERVICES
Ambulance/Fire/Police
T 191
Tourist police
T 1155
24-hour pharmacy
Foodland Supermarket Pharmacy
1413 Sukhumvit/Soi 5
T 02 254 2247

EMBASSIES
British Embassy
14 Thanon Wittayu
T 02 305 8333
ukinthailand.fco.gov.uk
US Embassy
120-22 Thanon Wittayu
T 02 273 5500
bangkok.usembassy.gov

MONEY
American Express
SP Building, 388 Thanon Phahonyothin
T 02 273 5500
travel.americanexpress.com

POSTAL SERVICES
Post office
Thanon Charoen Krung
T 02 233 1050
Shipping
DHL Express
1634/4 Thanon Phetchaburi Tat Mai
T 02 684 8200

BOOKS
Architects 49: Selected and Current Works edited by Kate Ryan and Eliza Hope (Images Publishing)
Classic Thai: Design Interiors Architecture by Chami Jotisalikorn and Phuthorn Bhumadhon (Tuttle Publishing)

WEBSITES
Architecture/design
aecasia.com
bangkokdesignfestival.com
Newspaper
bangkokpost.com

COST OF LIVING
Taxi from Suvarnabhumi International Airport to city centre
THB350
Cappuccino
THB100
Packet of cigarettes
THB75
Daily newspaper
THB35
Bottle of champagne
THB6,000

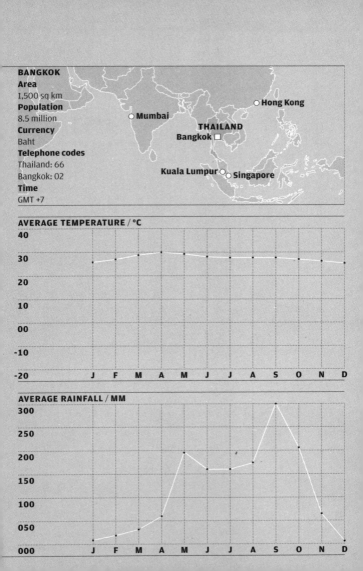

BANGKOK
Area
1,500 sq km
Population
8.5 million
Currency
Baht
Telephone codes
Thailand: 66
Bangkok: 02
Time
GMT +7

Mumbai

Hong Kong

THAILAND
Bangkok □

Kuala Lumpur ○ Singapore

AVERAGE TEMPERATURE / °C

40
30
20
10
00
-10
-20
J F M A M J J A S O N D

AVERAGE RAINFALL / MM

300
250
200
150
100
050
000
J F M A M J J A S O N D

NEIGHBOURHOODS
THE AREAS YOU NEED TO KNOW AND WHY

To help you navigate the city, we've chosen the most interesting districts (see the map inside the back cover) and underlined featured venues in colour, according to their location (see below); those venues that are outside these areas are not coloured.

CHATUCHAK

In the north of the city, this area is centred on the wooden sprawl of the world-famous Chatuchak Weekend Market (or 'JJ') and the little-known Chatuchak Park. Heading out here are the SkyTrain, from which you get a great view of the Elephant Building (see p066), and the MRT, the latter more convenient for the market. You'll also find one of the city's best food markets and vibrant, if off-the-radar, nightlife.

OLD TOWN

This district begins where the wide lanes of Thanon Sathorn reach the nut-brown Chao Phraya River. Here, hotels such as the Shangri-La (see p020) rise up with an imperious garishness, while further north, the sector that contains old wooden Chinese architecture and teeming noodle vendors marks the de facto Old Town. It's a mix of ancient and bustling modern, from the hidden Hokkien coffee shops to the boutique fashion stores.

SUKHUMVIT

This traffic-clogged, mall-mobbed avenue goes on for miles. It contains plenty of trendy sub-sections, whether that be leafy lanes such as Soi 31, with its furniture and fashion studios, or urban it-spots such as Thong Lor and Ekamai (Soi 63) — all neighbourhoods unto themselves. Many eating, drinking and dancing hot spots are found round here, including Bo.lan (see p041) and Bed Supperclub (see p058).

SIAM

Students, high-haired society wives and even Lithuanian and Brazilian models flock to this shopping and youth-culture hub. All flow between the air-conditioned malls, such as the Siam Center (see p076), on the north side of Thanon Rama I, and the neon-lit lanes to the south. Rummaging in backstreet stalls will yield cheap jewellery and even a deco cinema, the Scala Theatre (T 02 251 2861).

SILOM AND SATHORN

Situated south-west of the city's lung, Lumphini Park (see p014), this is the one part of Bangkok with a linear concentration of skyscrapers, including the idiosyncratic Robot Building (see p013) and financial-powerhouse offices. The focus of the area tends to be the pedestrianised Thanon Silom and its sister side lanes, Convent and Sala Daeng, lined with gay bars, dance halls, destination eateries, such as D'Sens (see p048), and lady-boy cabarets.

ROYAL CITY AVENUE (RCA)

Once a students-only realm, with lurid massage parlours tucked down the nearby alleys, the RCA district has undergone a rapid facelift. The city officially shuts down at 1am but RCA is regularly open at least an hour later, and a fresh generation of owners with a global vision have made it a nightlife draw with a club for every taste, such as the dance palace Flix/Slim (29/22-32 Royal City Avenue, T 02 203 0377).

LANDMARKS

THE SHAPE OF THE CITY SKYLINE

Bangkok is a textbook example of urban Asian sprawl. It has many concrete, six-lane avenues in the wrong parts of town and one-lane avenues in the right ones. However, if you break the city down by how you want to shop, work and play, it can be manageable.

Shopping happens mostly along one long, smoggy strip that begins by Siam Square and unfurls along the path of the SkyTrain. Thanon Sukhumvit begins roughly around the area occupied by the sleazy Nana Plaza complex. Its side lanes, or *soi*, can be like mini-neighbourhoods; key numbers include Soi 63, or Ekamai, hub of the local party scene, and Soi 55, aka Thong Lor, for its abundance of spas, architect Duangrit Bunnag's H1 (see p065) and high-end malls such as J Avenue (No 15) and Penny's Balcony (No 522/3).

The Old Town begins by the State Tower (1055 Thanon Silom), a 247m landmark designed by Thai firm Rangsan Architecture, and encompasses wooden shophouses, noodle-store-filled alleys and temples such as Wat Pho (Thanon Chetuphon) and the Royal Grand Palace (Thanon Na Phra Lan) along the banks of the Chao Phraya. The other areas to visit are Silom and Sathorn, a mash-up of offices, swish hotels, quaint sidestreets, A-list eateries and the sleaze of Patpong. Above all of this, the MahaNakhon Building is rising; when OMA's mostly residential tower is finished, perhaps as early as 2012, it will be Bangkok's tallest structure, at 313m high. *For full addresses, see Resources.*

CAT Building
The head office of CAT Telecom, this 35-floor tower sits on the edge of the Chao Phraya, from where it beams radio waves across the city. It's the kind of lumpen, glass-and-steel office block that gives new Asian architecture such a bad name, but it does make a useful reference point along the river, near the distinctive dome of the State Tower (pictured, right).
72 Thanon Charoen Krung

Dusit Thani

The tallest building in the city for at least a few months after its opening in 1970, this hotel is a rare project, reflecting art deco and modernist influences in a way that is distinctly Thai. Striking at night, when the geometrical, gold-lined frames that run up the structure are lit up, the hotel is symbolic to Bangkok residents because it is locally owned and was one of the first buildings in the city to make a high-rise statement. For expats, the fusion of Eastern elements in a Western modernist context is the point of conversation. Note the influence of Buddhist architecture in the portico-like frames and shape of the structure. Lumphini Park (see p014) starts within a few steps of its doors.
946 Thanon Rama IV, T 02 200 9000, dusit.com

Robot Building

At ground level, there is not a great deal to distinguish the Bangkok headquarters of the United Overseas Bank (UOB) from any other high-rise lining the gridlocked Sathorn Road. However, viewed from afar (the SkyTrain between Surasak and Chong Nonsi stations, say), Bangkok architect Sumet Jumsai's 83m-high structure jumps out. Tagged the 'Robot', it was inspired by one of his son's toys and completed in 1986. The staggered shape rises through 20 floors, its 6m-diameter 'eyeballs' of reflective glass forming windows, hooded by metal-louvred 'eyelids'. The rooftop communication antennae serve as lightning rods and the 'caterpillar wheels' and reinforced concrete 'nuts' adorning the building also have a practical function as window casings and sunshades.

191 Thanon Sathorn Tai

Lumphini Park
Formerly royal property, this park was opened to the public in the 1920s and remains the city's one true, readily used expanse of grass, ponds and shady paths. Backgammon is played under pagodas, and elsewhere you'll see locals engaging in aerobics, badminton, yoga, ballroom dancing, jogging, football and the Thai sport *takraw*, a kind of kick volleyball.
Thanon Rama IV

HOTELS

WHERE TO STAY AND WHICH ROOMS TO BOOK

If there is any one business that benefits from the no worry/all smiles Thai approach to life and the fluid grace of Buddhist society, it is hospitality. First-time visitors to Bangkok may appreciate the relative tranquillity of the river, where five-star choices abound, from the grande dame of local hotels, the Mandarin Oriental (48 Thanon Charoen Krung/Soi 38, T 02 659 9000), to the plush Shangri-La (see p020). Of the other riverside retreats, The Peninsula (see p024) and the Millennium Hilton (123 Thanon Charoen Nakorn, T 02 442 2000) are good options; for a more intimate experience, we recommend the elegant Arun Residence (see p026).

Downtown, there is a trend towards design-conscious refits, such as Siam@Siam (see p022), Dream (opposite) and the smallest of the three, Luxx XL (82/8 Soi Lang Suan, T 02 684 1111), a 51-room conversion of a seven-storey building on hip Soi Lang Suan. Designed by owner Dusadee Srishevachart, it features a 12m salt-system infinity pool. The global economic crisis does not appear to have halted the arrival of several new properties in the city. A 37-storey Radisson (36 Thanon Narathivatratchanakarin, T 02 210 9000) opened in December 2009, while a 400-room W Hotel, designed by Palmer & Turner, is due in 2011. The MahaNakhon Building (see p009) will house a 150-room Edition hotel, a collaboration between Ian Schrager and Marriott.
For full addresses and room rates, see Resources.

Dream

This boutique hotel, owned by socialite Vikram Chatwal, was converted in 2006 from an existing building by Bent Severin. The interiors, by Bangkok firm ASC, follow a modern, East-meets-West aesthetic; the lobby (overleaf) features replicas of the mound-like *chedi* found in Buddhist temples. The 195 rooms are bathed in a relaxing blue-hued light from recessed fluorescent tubes situated in glass desktops and under the platform beds, as in the stylish Dream Suite 807 (above). Techno-furnishings include an iPod Nano, DVD player, free wi-fi and a 42in plasma TV. Dream is popular with creative types who appreciate the high-quality service, the bar/lounge Flava (see p060) and the rooftop pool parties in the Dream 2 wing. *10 Sukhumvit Soi 15, T 02 254 8500, dreambkk.com*

Lobby, Dream

Shangri-La Hotel

Set on the banks of the Chao Phraya, the 799-room Shangri-La – opened in 1986, and given a £36m makeover in 2009 – has enough facilities for you never to feel the need to leave. Indeed, many of its guests shuttle only between their rooms and their respective business meetings in the city. The accommodation, divided between two wings, is plush, comfortable and well equipped – we were taken with the view from the Speciality Suite (above). The complex includes five restaurants, serving Thai, Cantonese, Italian and global fare, and three bars. Recuperate in the health club or the CHI spa, the most luxurious in the city, where the 107 sq m Garden Suite has an outdoor infinity bath set in a lotus pond. Also look out for the lovely swimming pools hidden among the manicured, if slightly twee, gardens.
89 Soi Wat Suan Plu, T 02 236 7777, shangri-la.com/bangkok

Siam@Siam Design Hotel & Spa
This 203-room hotel with an extensive
spa opened in 2007, its bold orange
and blue façade contrasting with the
raw concrete walls and steel accents
favoured by interior designer Kittisak
Suthammachote. Rooms, such as the
Grand Biz Class (pictured), feature
abstract paintings by local artists.
865 Thanon Rama I, T 02 217 3000,
www.siamatsiam.com

The Peninsula

This 39-storey hotel, opened in 1998, more than matches its celebrated Hong Kong counterpart and, with its modern delivery of Old World class, rivals the Mandarin Oriental (T 02 659 9000) over the water. We like the almost painfully energetic service, the panoramic vistas of the city and the admittedly gaudy but supremely comfortable Thai Suite (above). The Pen scores heavily over other big riverfront properties thanks to slick touches, such as a dramatic, three-tiered Romanesque pool that runs down to the river (part of the hotel's lavish ESPA spa, opened in 2006) and cultural investment in an impressive Asian art collection. A speedy river-shuttle service for guests leaves from the Peninsula Pier Lounge, from 6am to midnight.
333 Thanon Charoen Nakorn,
T 02 861 2888, peninsula.com

Mayfair Marriott

Long or short stay, one of Bangkok's in-the-know lodging options for maximum comfort and minimum fuss is the wide range of serviced apartments. Those at the Mayfair Marriott offer all the perks of going super deluxe – business centre, broadband, dedicated concierge, technical assistance, indoor pool with stunning views (above), 24-hour gym – without the prying and peeping of doting staff.

The One-Bedroom Suite has a fluffy king-sized bed, a living room with a large desk, and a well-equipped kitchen. The staff will try to meet your every request, from buying local SIM cards to securing tables at restaurants or clubs.
60 Lang Suan Soi, T 02 263 9333, marriott.com

Arun Residence
Portuguese-colonial-style architecture coexists with Ratanakosin-era Thai art at this boutique hotel, opened in 2005. The renovation of a former waterfront warehouse was overseen by Thai architect and interior designer Chawalit Chawawan, who has created a simply decorated, two-storey, six-room hideaway on the banks of the Chao Phraya. We recommend you book the spacious Roof Garden Suite (right). Outside the air-conditioned rooms it can get rather stuffy, but this only adds to the authentic ambience – the hotel is located in a tiny one-lane *soi* filled with shophouses selling everything from metal panelling to rice. The breathtaking views of Wat Arun (see p034) are best at sunrise and at dusk, while enjoying Thai fusion cuisine at the Deck by the River restaurant on Arun's wooden veranda.
36-38 Soi Pratoo Nok Yoong, T 02 221 9158, arunresidence.com

Chakrabongse Villas

This urban retreat takes its name from a Thai prince, who built these Ayutthaya-style stilted wooden villas for entertaining back in 1908. The four apartments – the Thai House, the Riverside Villa, the Garden Suite (above) and the Chinese Suite – have an intimacy that recalls European-style inns on a good day. The apartments have luxurious beds, polished floors, darkwood fittings and traditional Thai furnishings.

Among the amenities are a 10m pool, a chef who heads to market daily and takes all requests, and a private boat mooring. As with the Arun Residence (see p026), you can see Wat Arun across the water and, unlike in the five-star waterfront hotels, there is a sense of engagement with the rituals and rhythms of daily Thai life.
396 Thanon Maharat, T 02 622 3356, thaivillas.com

Metropolitan

Christina Ong's urban hostelry is a former YMCA, and its featureless architecture was used as a blank canvas, as you may detect from the lobby (above). The exterior is lit in glowing panels by Isometrix's Arnold Chan, so the double-height duplex Penthouse Suites are as alluring from the outside as they are within. Staff flit about in Comme des Garçons threads and rooms feature yoga mats and teak lotus chairs; we suggest you opt for the Metropolitan Room (overleaf) or a Terrace Room, which have semi-outdoor showers. Darkwoods offset a Zen-touched minimalism in the COMO Shambala Spa, and hotel guests are welcomed in the members-only Met Bar (see p045). Note that the blue-tiled pool only gets sunlight around lunchtime. *27 Thanon Sathorn Tai, T 02 625 3333, metropolitan.como.bz*

Metropolitan Room, Metropolitan

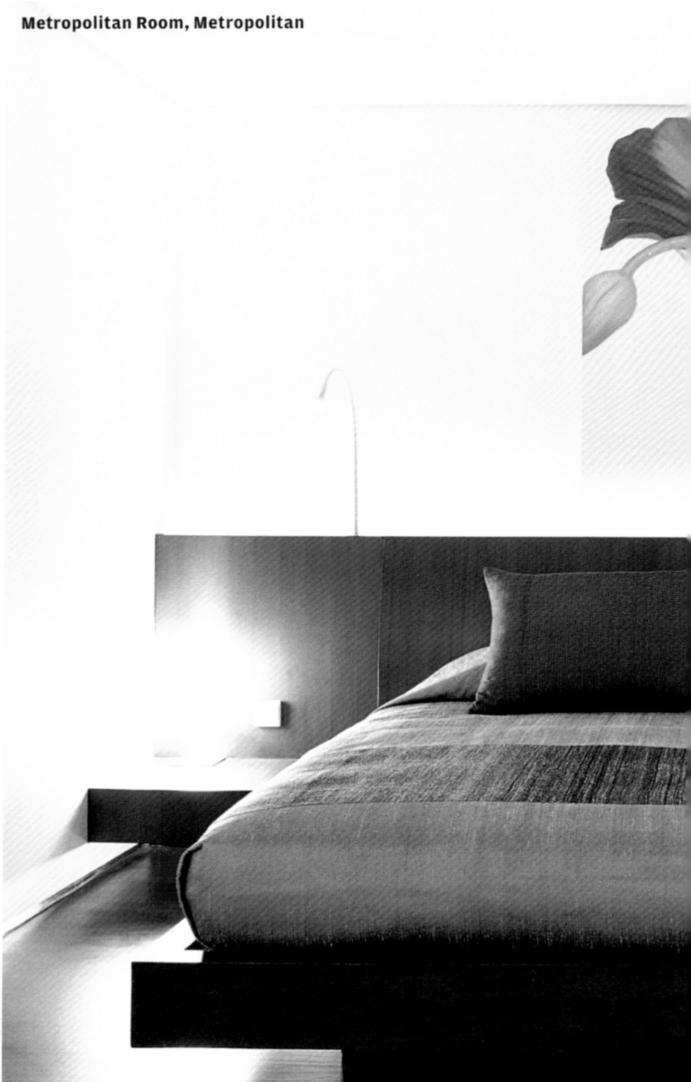

24 HOURS

SEE THE BEST OF THE CITY IN JUST ONE DAY

Fifteen years ago, Bangkok had fewer than 100 7-Eleven stores and not a public-transport system or eight-lane highway in sight. The thought of trying to see the city in 24 hours would send shudders through wide-eyed tourists and knowing locals alike. A three-hour trip from the airport was standard, and it took two hours to get from Lumphini Park (see p014) to Chinatown. But things have changed. Now, as well as the old methods of transport, such as boats and motorbikes, there are the MRT and the SkyTrain – its long-awaited airport extension is due for completion in 2011.

The City of Angels is a city of extremes and to explore it properly, you should experience them all: on land and on water; from high society down to grass-roots level; and from the royal palaces to the dizzying, fume-filled streets. This means greeting the day with a coffee, as the locals do, perhaps at the refined Erawan (opposite), before a trip down the Chao Phraya. Above all, it means having fun and not forgetting to relax; if the boat ride doesn't do it, then a massage at Ruen-Nuad (2nd floor, 42 Thanon Convent, T 02 632 2662), located in a charming traditional wooden house, or Thann Sanctuary Spa (see p094) surely will. End the day with dinner and drinks at one of Bangkok's myriad rooftop venues such as The Roof (see p038). This is the land of *sanuk* (a Thai word that loosely translates as 'fun') and *mai pen rai* (basically, 'don't worry').
For full addresses, see Resources.

09.00 Erawan Tea Room

Located on the second floor of the stylish Erawan Bangkok shopping mall (T 02 250 7777), Erawan Tea Room is a legendary 1960s venue, where Jackie Kennedy is reputed to have dined. The interior was reinvented by designer Tony Chi, with warm orange tones and Thai-Chinese detailing. It's a pleasant place for morning coffee. Sit near the windows, if you can, which overlook the Erawan Shrine, a gilded statue erected in the 1950s to appease the land gods during the building of the Erawan Hotel, now the Grand Hyatt Erawan (T 02 254 1234). If you prefer tea to coffee, you can choose from Indian, Sri Lankan, Chinese or Thai (the teas are also available packaged to take away).
494 Thanon Ploenchit, T 02 250 7777, www.erawanbangkok.com

10.30 Wat Arun Temple

Two different faces of Bangkok can be seen on the banks of the Chao Phraya, with Sino-Portuguese shophouses looking across to shiny, modern hotels. Take a river taxi from Saphan Taksin pier for the 15-minute ride to Tha Tien, past locals fishing for their dinner. From here an express boat will ferry you to Wat Arun. The temple's towering central prang is surrounded by four smaller ones. Construction began during the Ayutthaya era (1350-1767), although the central prang wasn't added until the 19th century. Wat Arun is known as the Temple of the Dawn because of the way light shimmers off its stucco-covered surface, which is decorated with porcelain that had been used as ballast and discarded by Chinese ships. *34 Thanon Arun Amarin, T 02 891 1149*

13.00 Thailand Creative & Design Center

Opened in 2005, the Thailand Creative & Design Center (TCDC) hosts eclectic exhibitions, and its library (above) has more than 25,000 titles covering all aspects of design, including art history, architecture, fashion and photography. Duangrit Bunnag designed the space using local teak for the bookshelves, and a gold motif typically seen in Thai temples. When you're done with the culture, have lunch at Bharani@TCDC (T 02 664 8468), an outlet of Bharani (T 02 260 1626), one of the first restaurants to serve Western food in Bangkok. If you don't fancy the crispy beef taco pizza, the boat noodles are a speciality. The Emporium Complex, which houses TCDC, opened in 1997, and was designed by Parisian firm J+H Boiffils. *6th floor, Emporium Shopping Complex, T 02 664 8448, tcdc.or.th*

PURE ESSENTIAL OILS · CANDLES · INCENSES · DRY PERFUMES

15.30 Karmakamet

Co-owners Sommart Pitakkingtong and Natthorn Rakchana launched Karmakamet as an interiors stall at Jatujak Market in 2001. Expanding into fragrances for the home and body, they opened this flagship store in 2007, where you'll find beautifully packaged perfumes for both men and women that blend buddleia, Siamese gardenia, millingtonia and frangipani with Indo-Chinese and Western flowers.

Rakchana furnished the interior with dark teak and brass cabinets and two brass and gold-leaf chandeliers. A range of more than 50 herbal, floral and fruit teas, and homemade Thai treats such as *kanom kleeb lamduan* (aromatic cookies) and *kanom pia* (crunchy coconut balls) are available at the in-store tea room (above). *2nd floor, Zone C, Central World, T 02 613 1397, karmakamet.co.th*

20.00 The Roof Restaurant

One of Bangkok's best rooftop venues is
the alfresco restaurant at the Siam@Siam
Hotel (see p022), where you can grill your
ribeye or ostrich steak yourself on slabs
of volcanic stone. Kittisak Suthammachote's
industrial design features stainless-steel
balconies and wire-mesh seating, allowing
360-degree views of the neon skyline.
*25th floor, Siam@Siam Hotel, 865 Thanon
Rama I, T 02 217 3070, siamatsiam.com*

URBAN LIFE
CAFÉS, RESTAURANTS, BARS AND NIGHTCLUBS

Although the persistent intervention of the Thai government has partly neutered the city's one-time wild nightlife, Bangkok is still the most vibrant South-East Asian capital in which to eat, drink, dance and attempt all combinations in-between. And wherever you are in the city, superb, spicy Thai food can be found on nearly every street corner. Or try bird's nest soup, dim sum or shark fin soup around the night markets of Chinatown (Thanon Yaowarat).

Iconic sip-and-sup spots, such as Bed Supperclub (see p058) and Met Bar (see p045), are still on the itinerary, despite similar hip upstarts generally falling out of favour after six months. However, entire areas, such as Thanon Sarasin, have developed extremely stylish local scenes. Silom 4 is the centre of gay Bangkok, and Thanon Ari has benefited from an influx of young professionals looking for stylish condos and an address in the heart of the city.

Closer to the city's Siamese roots are the wood-clad whisky bars favoured by artists, students and politicians slumming it. The Old Town district is a popular hangout, while Thong Lor and Ekamai are where the beautiful children of the country's leaders squander their trust funds. Royal City Avenue (RCA) is a reborn club/bar strip that stays open late on the right nights and has a come-one-come-all spirit that hints that the Bangkok of old might just return and merge with what we love about the new one.
For full addresses, see Resources.

Bo.lan

Former students of David Thompson, the Michelin-starred chef at Nahm in London, Duangporn Songvisava (Bo) and Dylan Jones (lan) opened Bo.lan in 2009. The name is also a play on the Thai word *boran*, meaning 'ancient', and the menu would not be out of place in the courts of the Sukhothai and Ayutthaya periods. The fragrant, delicate taste of dishes such as *dtom gati* of white prawn and lotus shoot, and stir-fried squid with palm heart and flowering chive expertly showcase the impressive breadth of Thai cooking. The interior features traditional rattan, exquisite prints by artist Ekachai Prapanja and lampshades fashioned out of *gra dong* (traditional flat baskets made from bamboo used for drying chillies and fish). *42 Soi Pichai Ronnarong, Sukhumvit Soi 26, T 02 260 2962, bolan.co.th*

Long Table

Since opening in 2008, Long Table has
become one of the city's top nightspots.
An entrance corridor illuminated by
hundreds of spotlights leads you to
the main room and its 24m hard-teak
centrepiece, said to be the world's longest
dining table, which can seat up to 70
people. Conceived by the team behind
Bed Supperclub (see p058), here, too,
divans line the edges of the room, and
are frequented by Thai *hiso* and beautiful
jet-setters. Located 25 floors up, its
expansive windows give a view of
Benjakiti Park, and there is also an
outdoor terrace with a pool and cocktail
bar. The Thai cuisine is equally impressive
aesthetically, though it can seem a triumph
of style over substance.
Column Tower, Sukhumvit Soi 16,
T 02 302 2557, longtablebangkok.com

Sirocco

This chic venue takes its name from the Mediterranean wind, and serves dishes from the same region. Perched 209m up on the 63rd floor of the State Tower, Sirocco offers stunning vistas over the Chao Phraya and Thon Buri. It's at night that the bar/restaurant comes into its own. LEDs emit soft hues of blue, pink and green, and a large dome, which can be seen halfway across the city, provides an illuminated backdrop to the alfresco dining. For non-vertigo-sufferers, a skywalk stretches out over the city, on which there is a circular bar (above), serving fine wine and premium vodka. Sirocco is renowned for hosting glitzy, big-budget dinners for the Thai élite, but tends to close at the first sign of rain. *Lebua at State Tower, 1055 Thanon Silom, T 02 624 9999, thedomebkk.com*

Met Bar

Set inside the Metropolitan hotel (see p029), this members-only bar (unless you're staying at the hotel) opened in 2003 and caters to incoming foreigners, Thai high society and the odd rock star and Hollywood actress. The striking interior by Singapore designer Kathryn Kng features furniture by Koichiro Ikebuchi (formerly of Japanese firm Super Potato) and artwork from Sydney-based multimedia artist Murray Hilton. Sink back into one of the black leather chaises longues and order a passion-fruit vodka martini or the Met's signature Tom Yumtini, which is based on the Thai soup and made with galangal-infused vodka, lemongrass and chilli.
27 Thanon Sathorn Tai, T 02 625 3399, www.metropolitan.como.bz/bangkok

Ruen Mallika
Dining in a 180-year-old teak house
is something you should do at least once
in Bangkok. The menu at Ruen Mallika
sweeps from the fiery cooking of south
Thailand to royal household curries. But
it is the delicate flowers in the garden
and the antiques strewn inside that
truly transport. Recline on a triangular
'axe cushion' for the full experience.
189 Sukhumvit Soi 22, T 02 663 3211

D'Sens

Ever since 2004, Bangkok foodies have
flocked to the top floor of the Dusit Thani
hotel (see p012) for a table at D'Sens,
an outpost of acclaimed chefs Jacques and
Laurent Pourcel, who create 'new French
cuisine with Mediterranean influences'.
Designer Imaad Rahmouni has set an
appropriate stage for this culinary treat.
Diners enter the restaurant past a curtain
of hand-crafted glass beads to be seated
in booths with leather banquettes and
comfy chairs that gently rock on striped
Paul Smith carpets. Oversized aquariums
are filled with tropical fish – an Asian
symbol of opulence and certainly not for
eating – and, as if that were not visual
stimulation enough, the views of the city
and Lumphini Park from the restaurant
and bar (right), where people head after
dinner, are particularly impressive.
Dusit Thani, 946 Thanon Rama IV,
T 02 200 9000, dusit.com

Hazara

Bangkok's role as a centre for Asian dining is often overlooked; Chinese, Vietnamese and Indian cuisine are its strengths. Hazara specialises in northern Indian fare, but also features southern and Punjabi dishes, and its richly spiced curries (the king prawn comes highly recommended), tandoor roasts, pulled lamb and black dahl could hold their own almost anywhere on the subcontinent.

A tilted teak building (part of the Face Bangkok complex), Hazara opened in 2003 and was hand-built in the Ayutthaya style by woodworkers, yet also features modern furniture, Hindu and Balinese antiques and an assortment of relics. It attracts a mainly business crowd during the week – make reservations for dinner.
29 Sukhumvit Soi 38, T 02 713 6048, facebars.com

Nest

Concealed amid a forest of skyscrapers, the chilled-out hotel restaurant/bar Nest is an open-air oasis in the clubland of Sukhumvit Soi 11. Opened in 2008, the garden setting, complete with shera wood decking and tropical plants, is a great spot to kick back on a curved-framed bed. The menu is a mishmash of Thai, Western, Asian fusion and tapas-style dishes – unusual outside the five-star hotels – and from the cocktail list we recommend The Thailand, a sour-and-spicy *tom yam*, vodka, coconut and lime concoction. In the event of rain, a 50m retractable canvas roof extends over the space. Nest is popular with expats, trendy Thais and disco divas.
8th floor, Le Fenix Sukhumvit Hotel, 33/33 Sukhumvit Soi 11, T 02 305 4000, lefenix-sukhumvit.com

Zense

Situated atop the Zen department store (see p072) in the Central World shopping centre, Zense is one of Bangkok's most popular rooftop bars. Its size is an asset, giving sweeping sunset vistas. The muted design features tones of latte and black, and there are black bucket chairs, white daybeds, beanbags, woven water-hyacinth chairs and love seats strewn around. Unfortunately placed staircases block the sight lines on one side of the bar but the young crowd doesn't seem to mind, focusing instead on drinking cocktails and sharing plates of food from the five kitchens. Choose from modern Indian cuisine, such as lobster masala, Italian, Japanese fusion and, of course, Thai.
17th floor, Zen, Central World, T 02 100 9898, zensebangkok.com

Koi Restaurant

This LA-bred Japanese restaurant/lounge continues to provide the city with global glam – surprisingly, for such a hip spot, Koi's kudos has not waned since its 2005 launch, perhaps because it's such a handsome venue. Open-box architecture mixes Japanese-style quiet with tropical warmth, and the ordinary furniture is redeemed by being predominantly black and red. Sliver-thin gardens separate the bar from the sushi bar/restaurant, which offers a Californian-tinged Japanese menu. In 2007, Italian restaurant The Bridge also opened in this complex, set in a steel-and-glass pyramid. Both are closed Mondays. *26 Sukhumvit Soi 20, T 02 258 1590, koirestaurant.com*

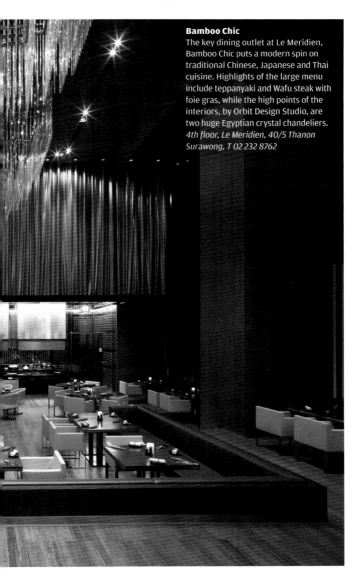

057 | URBAN LIFE

Bamboo Chic
The key dining outlet at Le Meridien,
Bamboo Chic puts a modern spin on
traditional Chinese, Japanese and Thai
cuisine. Highlights of the large menu
include teppanyaki and Wafu steak with
foie gras, while the high points of the
interiors, by Orbit Design Studio, are
two huge Egyptian crystal chandeliers.
*4th floor, Le Meridien, 40/5 Thanon
Surawong, T 02 232 8762*

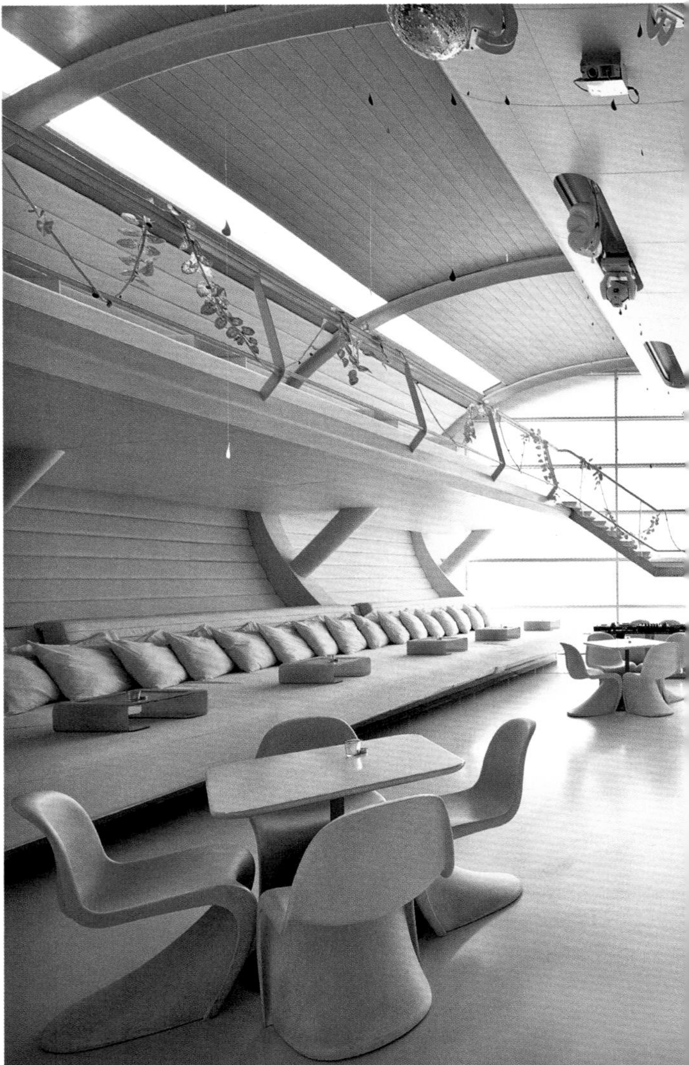

Bed Supperclub
Its white interior and curvaceous take on industrial design have made this tubular structure something of an archetypal venue for modern Bangkok. You can dine horizontally in the restaurant, choosing from a Mediterranean-Asian menu, and then boogie vertically in the adjoining club. *26 Sukhumvit Soi 11, T 02 651 3537, bedsupperclub.com*

Flava Lounge

This bar/lounge adds a little sex appeal to its host venue, Dream (see p017), the hotel whose cheeky interiors blend all things Asian and glam. Flava also offers a good list of cocktails, including lots of tempting concoctions with a local twist; try a Sly Thai (kiwi-flavoured vodka, Limoncello, lychee and kaffir lime leaf) or a Siamese Mule (passionfruit vodka, fresh ginger and lemongrass syrup).

Flava's resident or guest DJs liven things up later on with eclectic sets ranging from salsa to house. The bar also hosts themed music nights once a month.
10 Sukhumvit Soi 15, T 02 254 8500, dreambk.com

INSIDER'S GUIDE
PAULA TAYLOR, MODEL AND ACTRESS

From modelling to starring in her own sitcom, *Neu Koo Bra-doo Tup Bai*, VJ-ing on Channel V, and breaking into Hollywood in *Shadows*, Paula Taylor, who was raised by a British father and Thai mother, is one of Thailand's most-loved celebrities. 'There is something for everyone in Bangkok,' she says. 'It's so open-minded.'

Taylor likes to breakfast at Erawan Tea Room (see p033), and for a hearty lunch, she heads to The Cup Restaurant & Tea Room (193/21-22 Thanon Ratchadaphisek, T 02 264 0247). If the weather's not too hot, it's down to Ratchada Soi 26, and the street vendor Kil Kil Tay for Korean BBQ, cooked Thai style. For afternoon tea, she recommends Agalico (Sukhumvit Soi 51, T 02 662 5857).

'Thai designers are the most creative in Asia,' says Taylor, who is a big fan of the city's shopping scene. She suggests the boutiques Greyhound (Siam Paragon, T 02 129 4358) and Stretsis (Gaysorn Plaza, T 02 656 1125), both of which carry their own fashion lines.

A night out may well start with a light dinner and drinks at the Banyan Tree's rooftop restaurant, Vertigo (21/100 Thanon Sathorn Tai, T 02 679 1200), and end with a midnight feast at Khao Thom Thong Lor 55 (Sukhumvit Soi 55), where she orders the signature fish on a sizzling plate. Or she'll head to Suan Malee (an area that translates as 'Jasmine Garden') for chicken fried noodles, before winding down with a cocktail at the Met Bar (see p045).
For full addresses, see Resources.

ARCHITOUR

A GUIDE TO BANGKOK'S ICONIC BUILDINGS

Of all the dirty, congested, unplanned metropolises in Asia, there are none more inspiring than Bangkok. Without the way in which its highways, municipal structures and 1960s bungalows all exist in a mad, buzzing pile, the city would not be where it is now: teetering on the verge of a new movement in design (and, one hopes, architecture). Like a honeycomb, modern Bangkok is chaotic at first, but well patterned from afar. The 18th- and 19th-century wooden homes and old palaces are remnants of the last fluid era in Thai architecture. Since then, Western and Thai elements have fused, a trend that reached its zenith in the Dusit Thani (see p012).

Malls may have become the new odes to monumentality, but places like Duangrit Bunnag's H1 (opposite) and the Face Bangkok complex (29 Sukhumvit Soi 38, T 02 713 6048) suggest a 'boutique' backlash. Even the 1990s boom, which resulted in some ghastly buildings, maintained a fun element with the Elephant Building (overleaf). Of more recent projects, the SkyTrain – which opened its first two lines in 1999 – stands out for its transformation of urban space, while forthcoming additions to Bangkok's skyline include the MahaNakhon Building (see p009) and Raimon Land's 73-floor residential development The River; both are due for completion in 2012. For now, the city may lack great architecture, but it does force one to see things differently, and in a very Thai context.
For full addresses, see Resources.

H1

Although many of his very best works are private or outside Bangkok – such as the tranquil Alila Cha-Am resort (T 032 709 555), 160km to the south – Duangrit Bunnag is fast becoming Thailand's first great modern architect. H1 is his reshaping of a mini-mall in the buzzy Thong Lor neighbourhood. At night, when the interlocking L-shaped structures are lit up, the open-box architecture makes this a great place to wander around. All the Bunnag signatures – the division of public and private space, the touch of tropical Zen, the incorporation of a centuries-old tree at the centre of the compound (above) – are there. To Die For (T 02 381 4714), an H1 restaurant and lounge with a courtyard, is a charming place from which to ponder the scene.
988 Sukhumvit Soi 55, T 02 381 4717

Elephant Building
A testament to the locals' appreciation of all things bright and eye-popping, Arun Chaiseri's 1997 Elephant Tower probably could not have been built anywhere else. Its leg-like pillars, which house offices and apartments, pinkish-grey exterior and cut-out eye might come across as gaudy elsewhere, but in a Thai context they have a camp, quirky appeal.
Thanon Phahon Yothin

Democracy Monument
Completed in 1939, the Democracy
Monument sits in the middle of a busy
roundabout commemorating Thailand's
first constitution, signed on 24 June
1932. To signify the date, each of the
four 'wings' stands 24m tall – their height
makes them a useful navigational aid
while you get your bearings in the city.
The traffic around the monument can
make it difficult to see it up close. The
design was by an Italian, Corrado Feroci,
who became a Thai citizen and was even
credited with launching the country's
modern-art movement. His huge granite
statement became a rallying point for
civil unrest, and the tragic consequences
of protests in the 1970s and 1990s have
imbued it with a rather more solemn
impact than its creator intended.
Thanon Ratchadamnoen Klang/
Thanon Pracha Thipatai

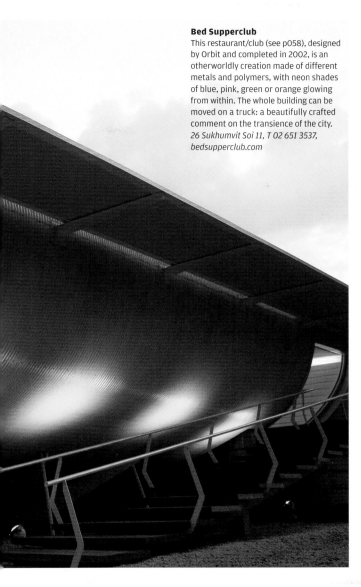

Bed Supperclub
This restaurant/club (see p058), designed
by Orbit and completed in 2002, is an
otherworldly creation made of different
metals and polymers, with neon shades
of blue, pink, green or orange glowing
from within. The whole building can be
moved on a truck: a beautifully crafted
comment on the transience of the city.
*26 Sukhumvit Soi 11, T 02 651 3537,
bedsupperclub.com*

SHOPPING

THE BEST RETAIL THERAPY AND WHAT TO BUY

Style has become Thailand's greatest form of modern capital. The fake Fendi and low-cost Lacoste that once pockmarked street markets seem finally to be on the wane. This has been helped by various government initiatives. The Thaksin administration (2001-2006) sought to promote the city as the fashion hub of South-East Asia, and the current one is investing heavily in film, graphic design and other creative industries. Global names-in-the-making include the architect Duangrit Bunnag and artist Jakkai Siributr. Other emerging players include H Ernest Lee, owner of H Gallery (201 Sathorn Soi 12, T 08 1310 4428) and Bhanu Inkawat, the menswear designer for the modish lifestyle brand Greyhound (see p062), which also incorporates a chain of popular, industrial-style cafés. Also making an impact is London-based graphic designer Pomme Chan, who contributed to the wallpaper for Microsoft's Windows 7.

The strongest crafts to seek out include jewellery, whether it's the ethnic drama of Kit-Ti (659 Baan Silom, T 08 1821 1275) or the society jewels of Lotus Arts de Vivre (41/21 Thanon Rama III, T 02 294 1821); minimalist, earthen ceramics; and all things graphic. Retail outlets are often destinations in themselves, from the outrageous mash-up of It's Happened To Be A Closet (266/3 Siam Square Soi 3, T 02 658 4696) to the upscale complexes H1 (see p065) and Zen department store (Central World, T 02 100 9999). *For full addresses, see Resources.*

Vanilla Garden

Visaka 'Jom' Raiva's Vanilla Garden is a converted 1930s house that's now home to two restaurants and the Sauce bookshop. The store has a double-height glass front and is set beside a pristine garden, at the centre of which sits a tall fountain. The interior houses hard-to-find and specialist tomes, from architecture in modern China to Indian cooking, and wealthy students and the wives of Japanese expats can be found browsing here. The complex also houses the 1950s-style Vanilla Café, which serves hearty Japanese fare and pâtisserie, and the traditional Chinese tea house Royal Vanilla, where diners eat dim sum seated on wooden stools.
53 Ekamai Soi 12/Sukhumvit Soi 63,
T 02 381 6120

Asava
Thai designer Polpat Asavaprapha's
fashion brand, Asava, caters to female
urbanites, with day-to-night pieces
in fabrics such as duchesse satin and
organza. Multiple mirrored prisms
covering the entrance and back wall
of his flagship store, designed by Thai
firm MA Studio, create a collage effect.
*1st floor, Siam Paragon, 991 Thanon
Rama I, T 02 6626 5267*

Siam Center

The student-mobbed Siam area is ground zero for fashion trends, which often start, live and die in shops the size of a compact hatchback. The Siam Center is the place to pick up globally recognised designer names, but those seeking up-and-coming labels will also find exclusive boutiques with individual takes on modern style, such as the street- and clubwear at SuperrZaaap!! (T 02 251 2142). Most of the more idiosyncratic shops are found on the third floor. Head for Senada (T 02 735 1267), Munchu (T 02 658 1134) and Baking Soda (above; T 02 251 5968), the women's line from Duangta Nantakwang, of clubwear label Soda.

Thanon Rama I, siampiwat.com

Lamont

Alexander Lamont founded his Bangkok workshop in 1999, and today the firm comprises a team of more than 80 artists, craftsmen and designers, specialising in Asian-influenced furniture and interior products with a craft background. The ceramic 'Royal Pumpkin Jars' (above) with an antique glaze, from 3,300 baht each, received a UNESCO Award of Excellence for Handicrafts in 2008. Lamont's flagship store opened in the same year. The interiors were designed by Hong Kong-based Peter Hunter Design and feature African granite floors and numerous mirrors. The centrepiece is a 4m jagged counter covered in gold leaf.

The Sukhothai Hotel, 13/3 Thanon Sathorn, T 02 287 3058, lamont-design.com

Propaganda
Opened in 1994, Propaganda is revered
for its cutting-edge product design.
The brand's trademark is glossy plastic
pieces with a humorous touch – many,
such as the stools shaped like molars,
are inspired by anatomy. The store is
dominated by a foam model of its chirpy
Mr P logo, which hangs from the roof.
4th floor, Siam Discovery Center,
Thanon Rama I, T 02 658 0430

Panta

Few had ever heard of water hyacinth until it began clogging up huge waterways like the Mekong and Amazon. Merging creativity with resourcefulness, the Thai design community took up the challenge of using this natural material as structural fodder and an entire movement was born. Panta opened in 2001, selling furniture and homewares wrought from this flexible weed, along with mauve celadon, wicker and items rooted in the local canals and jungles. Largely woven, pieces blend a touch of 1950s Scandinavian style with tropical organic shapes, and are exceptional buys, given the price. Panta's success led to the opening of a second store (T 02 129 4430) in the Siam Paragon mall in 2005.

4th floor, Siam Discovery Center, Thanon Rama I, T 02 658 0415, pantathailand.net

Harnn

When it comes to Thai-style wellbeing, it's hard to beat an indigenous massage, but the land of lemongrass has much more to offer the body. We picked up these all-natural soaps (above), 155 baht for 100g, by Harnn, a rapidly expanding local brand that is already stocked in 22 countries. Vitamin E-rich extracts of rice bran oil – an antioxidant with anti-ageing properties – provide the core ingredient for Harnn and sister brand Thann's (see p094) wide range of natural hair and skincare products for men and women. Harnn's flagship outlet in Siam Paragon opened in 2005 and was designed by managing director Vudhichai Harnphanich, who was inspired by the look of traditional herbal medicine shops.
4th floor, Siam Paragon, 991/1 Thanon Rama I, T 02 610 9715, harnn.com

Flynow
Few Thai brands can boast the success of Flynow, which launched in 1983 and now has numerous outlets in Bangkok. Recent collections combined sportswear with a feminine aesthetic, but Flynow's trademarks are classic black-and-white designs, and leatherwear. This store in Central World has an antique-wood finish.
Central World, 4/5 Thanon Ratchadamri, T 02 646 1037, flynowbangkok.com

Almeta

Though most people flock to the Jim Thompson House (T 02 216 7368) in their blind, giddy rush to check silk-buying off their shopping lists, several more personal (and singular in what they offer, in terms of style) alternatives are more in line with the current Bangkok trends. Almeta is a one-stop shopping affair for bespoke silk design that has been going strong since 1992. Customers can choose any combination of weave, ply, weight or colour they desire and normally receive their product within days. All items are hand-woven by request in Isaan, Thailand's north-eastern region.

20/3 Sukhumvit Soi 23, T 02 258 4227, almeta.com

Qconceptstore
Covering 500 sq m of the Siam Paragon mall, Qconceptstore opened in 2006 and purveys a hotchpotch of retro toys and arts and crafts, hipster fashion by up-and-coming Thai designers and furniture imported from Europe, including the German brand Kare. The rather garish interior was designed by Thai firm IAW.
Siam Paragon, 991 Thanon Rama I,
T 02 610 9540, qconceptstore.com

SPORTS AND SPAS

WORK OUT, CHILL OUT OR JUST WATCH

As chaotic and sweltering as Bangkok can be, there are calmer intervals, when pockets of breeze and a gorgeous light make for a great time to exercise. Tennis has become very popular, on the heels of the now-struggling Paradorn Srichaphan, who was the first Asian player to break into the world's top 10, in 2003. Gym time is a priority for the locals and places such as Cascade Club (6th-7th floor, Ascott Sathorn Hotel, 187 Thanon Sathorn Tai, T 02 676 6969) and California WOW (Siam Paragon, 991 Thanon Rama I, T 02 627 5999) are scenes unto themselves. Yoga and Pilates classes continue to boom, and are affordable, whether you head to Lumphini Park (see p014) at 8am or to one of the many handsome studios, such as Yoga Elements (23rd floor, Vanissa Building, 29 Soi Chidlom, T 02 655 5671).

Thai boxing is a bloody, gymnastic spectacle and a centrepiece of Siamese culture; the best place to watch it is Ratchadamnoen Stadium (1 Thanon Ratchadamnoen Nok, T 02 281 4205). Golf is also hugely popular, and visitors who want to tee off should head to Muang Ake Golf Club (52 Moo 7, Thanon Phahonyothin, T 02 533 9335), which has very reasonable green fees and is located 30km from the centre in Pathum Thani. And who could forget the form that Bangkok has nearly perfected? When it comes to urban day spas and massages, there is nary a bad one to be had.

For full addresses, see Resources.

Divana Massage & Spa

Set within an idyllic tropical garden plot, Divana is housed in a converted two-storey wood-and-brick house. It opened in 2002 and mainly caters to foreigners, especially from Japan and Korea, keen to experience one of Asia's premier spa destinations. There are 11 individually designed Thai-style spa rooms, each with a private steam room and a small bath tub, as well as a dimly lit, teak-floored main area. Options include Siamese massage and a signature Champagne Mango body treatment, with prices ranging from around 950 baht to 4,350 baht for some of the all-day spa packages. Afterwards, relax with some herbal tea in the indoor air-conditioned Thai-style pavilion overlooking the gardens.
7 Sukhumvit Soi 25, T 02 661 6784, divanaspa.com

SF Strike Bowl

Bowling has been co-opted with extreme style in Bangkok. This particular outlet is secreted away near a food court on the hectic top floor of the MBK Center, but is of special interest because it was designed by Orbit Design Studio, the team behind Long Table (see p042) and Bed Supperclub (see p058). The highly graphic style and pale minimalism – incorporating wooden floors, greyish-blue walls and white ceilings – are quite similar here, with the décor adding a certain panache to the proceedings. There are pod-like karaoke booths, a DJ stage, lounge areas and even shoes specially designed by Orbit's creative team.

7th floor, MBK Center, Thanon Phaya Thai, T 02 611 4555

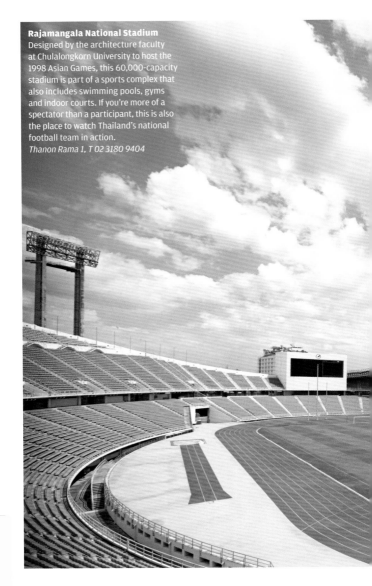

Rajamangala National Stadium
Designed by the architecture faculty
at Chulalongkorn University to host the
1998 Asian Games, this 60,000-capacity
stadium is part of a sports complex that
also includes swimming pools, gyms
and indoor courts. If you're more of a
spectator than a participant, this is also
the place to watch Thailand's national
football team in action.
Thanon Rama 1, T 02 3180 9404

Thann Sanctuary Spa

We've been buying Thann's natural wood-infused shower gels and jasmine-scented hand creams for years and were first in line when its spa opened in 2007. It offers a wide range of holistic treatments, including Ayurvedic head massage and a signature anti-oxidising treatment based on Shiso leaf extract. The interiors, a mix of Zen and tropical influences, are by founder Tony Suppattranont and designer Vitoon Kunalungkarn, with a dark-green-and-brown colour scheme supposed to evoke the rainforest, and a 6m-high ceiling adorned with 12,000 pieces of bamboo. The six low-lit treatment rooms are themed by the brand's product range – Rice, Aromatic Wood, Oriental Essence and so on – and are fragrant, moody and suitably sensuous. *Gaysorn Plaza, 999 Thanon Ploenchit, T 02 656 1424, thann.info*

ESCAPES
WHERE TO GO IF YOU WANT TO LEAVE TOWN

Paying due respect to the Thai love of extremes, if one leaves the sprawl and traffic of the city, it will most likely be for some kind of peace and a touch of nature. You could drive the 90 minutes north to the UNESCO World Heritage temples of Ayutthaya or head west, where the seven-level waterfalls of Erawan, idyllic river scenery and the Bridge on the River Kwai lure coachloads to Kanchanaburi. However, in our opinion, the best option is to do as most locals would when given the chance – go to the beach.

It isn't necessary to go all the way down to Koh Samui, Phuket or Koh Chang for tropical shorelines and exotic scenery. Bangkok is, after all, a port, and the placid Gulf of Thailand is just over an hour's drive away. Fishing villages, resorts and weekend towns abound. Head for Ko Samet, a beautiful island and national park to the south-east of the city that is, by turns, a party destination, quiet respite or family gathering place, depending on the visitor. Pack your mosquito repellent, though. For both convenience and style, the best destinations are Hua Hin (see p098) and the nearby town of Kui Buri (opposite); the former was once a fishing hamlet, but entered the spotlight when King Rama VII built a palace there. It has since become the Hamptons of Thailand, attracting a posh weekend crowd to its buzzy scene of great hotels, seaside dining venues, summer jazz festival and elephant polo tournament.
For full addresses, see Resources.

X2 Kui Buri

In recent years, the cluster of villages around the once sleepy town of Hua Hin have seen an influx of jet-setters. A number of cutting-edge resorts have moved further afield, first to beaches such as Pranburi and now to a pristine town called Kui Buri, three hours south of Bangkok. This is where you will find X2, the original outpost of this Thai design-led resort company. There are 23 villas, featuring bare rock and a glass front wall. Most have private pools, and four of the villas are right on the beachfront. A bar and restaurant offer sophisticated sustenance. *52 Moo 13, Aoi Noi, Muang, Prachuap Khiri Khan, T 032 601 412, x2resorts.com*

Anantara Hua Hin Resort & Spa
Larger resorts are often a no-go for the
discerning traveller, but Anantara won
us over with its understated style, cool
shady pools, excellent fitness facilities
and decadent private bath tubs. In an
area where all the spas are top-notch,
the Eastern-inspired treatments here
are some of the best we've tried.
43/1 Thanon Phetkasem Beach,
T 032 520 250, huahin.anantara.com

Samujana Villas, Koh Samui

Formerly a brash tourist trap, Koh Samui has managed to retain elements of an unspoilt tropical paradise, and now boasts an increasing number of high-end resorts, such as The Library (see p102). But for a more personal experience, rent your own villa. Completed in 2004, Samujana is a tiered complex that clings to a hillside in the north-east of Koh Samui, overlooking Koh Matlang. All 15 villas were designed by Bali-based architects Gfab, in a pared-down style. Opt for Samujana Villa 7 (above), which sleeps up to eight people in four bedrooms and has an open-plan dining area that gives onto an infinity pool. There is a maid service between 8am and 10pm, and a chef can also be provided if required.
Choeng Mon, Bo Phut, T 081 086 6562, samuiholidayhomes.com

The Library, Koh Samui
Opened on Chaweng Beach in 2007,
this hotel, the brainchild of interior
designer Tirawan Songsawat, is based
around a striking glass-fronted library
(pictured). The 13 Suites and 13 Studio
Cabins have a bold red, grey and white
colour scheme; plans for a 20-room
extension were announced in 2009.
*14/1 Moo 2, Chaweng Beach, Bo Phut,
T 07 742 2768, thelibrary.co.th*

NOTES

SKETCHES AND MEMOS

RESOURCES

CITY GUIDE DIRECTORY

A

Agalico 062
Sukhumvit Soi 51
T 02 662 5857 ext 111
agalico.co.th

Almeta 084
20/3 Sukhumvit Soi 23
T 02 258 4227
almeta.com

Asava 074
1st floor
Siam Paragon
991 Thanon Rama I
T 02 6626 5267

B

Baking Soda 076
3rd floor
Siam Center
Thanon Rama I
T 02 251 5968

Bamboo Chic 056
4th floor
Le Meridien
40/5 Thanon Surawong
T 02 232 8762
lemeridienhotelbangkok.com

Bed Supperclub 058
26 Sukhumvit Soi 11
T 02 651 3537
bedsupperclub.com

Bharani 036
96/14 Sukhumvit Soi 23
T 02 260 1626

Bharani@TCDC 036
6th floor
Emporium Shopping Complex
622 Sukhumvit Soi 24
T 02 664 8468
tcdc.or.th

Bo.lan 041
42 Soi Pichai Ronnarong
Sukhumvit Soi 26
T 02 260 2962
bolan.co.th

C

California WOW 088
Siam Paragon
991 Thanon Rama I
T 02 627 5999

Cascade Club 088
6th-7th floor
Ascott Sathorn Hotel
187 Thanon Sathorn Tai
T 02 676 6969
cascadeclubandspa.com

CAT Building 010
72 Thanon Charoen Krung

The Cup Restaurant & Tea Room 062
193/21-22 Thanon Ratchadaphisek
T 02 264 0247

D

Democracy Monument 068
Thanon Ratchadamnoen Klang/
Thanon Pracha Thipatai

Divana Massage & Spa 089
7 Sukhumvit Soi 25
T 02 661 6784
divanaspa.com

D'Sens 048
Dusit Thani
946 Thanon Rama IV
T 02 200 9000
dusit.com

Dusit Thani 012
946 Thanon Rama IV
T 02 200 9000
dusit.com

HOTELS

ADDRESSES AND ROOM RATES

Alila Cha-Am 065
Room rates:
double, from THB7,750
115 Moo 7
Tambol Bangkao
Amphur Cha-Am
T 032 709 555
alilahotels.com

Anantara Hua Hin Resort & Spa 098
Room rates:
double, from THB5,500
43/1 Thanon Phetkasem Beach
Hua Hin
T 032 520 250
huahin.anantara.com

Arun Residence 026
Room rates:
double, from THB3,500;
Roof Garden Suite, from THB5,500
36-38 Soi Pratoo Nok Yoong
T 02 221 9158
arunresidence.com

Chakrabongse Villas 028
Room rates:
Garden Suite, THB9,350;
Thai House, THB11,700;
Riverside Villa, THB15,200;
Chinese Suite, from THB26,900
396 Thanon Maharat
T 02 622 3356
thaivillas.com

Dream 017
Room rates:
double, THB12,500;
Dream Suite 807, THB40,000
10 Sukhumvit Soi 15
T 02 254 8500
dreambkk.com

The Library 102
Room rates:
Studio Cabin, from THB12,600;
Suite, from THB14,400
14/1 Moo 2
Chaweng Beach
Bo Phut
Koh Samui
T 07 742 2768
thelibrary.co.th

Luxx XL 016
Room rates:
double, from THB3,050
82/8 Soi Lang Suan
T 02 684 1111
luxxxl.com

Mandarin Oriental 016
Room rates:
double, THB16,600
48 Thanon Charoen Krung/Soi 38
T 02 659 9000
mandarinoriental.com/bangkok

Mayfair Marriott 025
Room rates:
One-Bedroom Suite, from THB4,350;
60 Lang Suan Soi
T 02 263 9333
marriott.com

Metropolitan 029
  Room rates:
  double, THB10,175;
  Metropolitan Room, THB12,500;
  Terrace Room, THB14,000;
  Penthouse Suite, THB31,300
  27 Thanon Sathorn Tai
  T 02 625 3333
  metropolitan.como.bz

Millennium Hilton 016
  Room rates:
  double, THB7,000
  123 Thanon Charoen Nakorn
  T 02 442 2000
  bangkok.hilton.com

The Peninsula 024
  Room rates:
  double, THB16,400;
  Thai Suite, THB52,650
  333 Thanon Charoen Nakorn
  T 02 861 2888
  peninsula.com

Radisson Hotel Sathorn 016
  Room rates:
  double, from THB8,400
  36 Thanon Narathivatratchanakarin
  T 02 210 9000
  radisson.com

Samujana Villas 100
  Room rates:
  Villa, from THB15,500;
  Samujana Villa 7, from THB15,500
  Choeng Mon
  Bo Phut
  Koh Samui
  T 081 086 6562
  samuiholidayhomes.com

Shangri-La Hotel 020
  Room rates:
  double, from THB9,100;
  Speciality Suite, from THB93,000
  89 Soi Wat Suan Plu
  T 02 236 7777
  shangri-la.com/bangkok

Siam@Siam Design Hotel & Spa 022
  Room rates:
  double, from THB6,300;
  Grand Biz Class, from THB8,300
  865 Thanon Rama I
  T 02 217 3000
  www.siamatsiam.com

X2 Kui Buri 097
  Room rates:
  villas, from THB4,000
  52 Moo 13
  Aoi Noi
  Muang
  Prachuap Khiri Khan
  Kui Buri
  T 032 601 412
  x2resorts.com

WALLPAPER* CITY GUIDES

Editorial Director
Richard Cook

Art Director
Loran Stosskopf
Editor
Rachael Moloney
Authors
Arglit Boonyai
Rob McKeown
Adam Renton
Deputy Editor
Jeremy Case
Managing Editor
Jessica Diamond

Chief Designer
Daniel Shrimpton
Designer
Lara Collins

Map Illustrator
Russell Bell

Photography Editor
Sophie Corben
Photography Assistant
Robin Key

Sub-Editors
Vicky McGinlay
Stephen Patience
Editorial Assistant
Ella Marshall

**Wallpaper* Group
Editor-in-Chief**
Tony Chambers
Publishing Director
Gord Ray

Wallpaper* ® is a
registered trademark
of IPC Media Limited

First published 2006
Second edition (revised
and updated) 2010
© 2006 and 2010 IPC
Media Limited

ISBN 978 0 7148 5614 8

PHAIDON

Phaidon Press Limited
Regent's Wharf
All Saints Street
London N1 9PA

Phaidon Press Inc
180 Varick Street
New York, NY 10014

Phaidon® is a registered
trademark of Phaidon
Press Limited

www.phaidon.com

A CIP Catalogue record for
this book is available from
the British Library.

Printed in China

PHOTOGRAPHERS

Alex Hill
Robot Building, p013
Dream, p017, pp018-019
Siam@Siam Design Hotel
& Spa, pp022-023
Arun Residence,
pp026-027
Wat Arun Temple,
pp034-035
Thailand Creative & Design
Center, p036
Karmakamet, p037
The Roof Restaurant,
pp038-039
Bo.lan, p041
Long Table, pp042-043
Sirocco, p044
Bamboo Chic, pp056-057
Paula Taylor, p063
Vanilla Garden, p073
Asava, pp074-075
Propaganda, pp078-079
Flynow, pp082-083
Qconceptstore, pp086-087
Divana Massage
& Spa, p089
Rajamangala National
Stadium, pp092-093

Jason Lang
Erawan Tea Room, p033
D'Sens, pp048-049
Hazara, p050
Zense, pp052-053
H1, p065
Siam Center, p076
Panta, p080
SF Strike Bowl, pp090-091

Jonathan Minster
Harnn, p081

Robert Polidori
CAT Building, pp010-011
Dusit Thani, p012
Shangri-La Hotel, p021
Elephant Building,
pp066-067
Democracy Monument,
pp068-069

Marc Schultz
Lumphini Park, pp014-015
Chakrabongse
Villas, p028
Met Bar, p045
Ruen Mallika, pp046-047
Nest, p051
Koi Restaraunt, pp054-055
Flava Lounge, pp060-061
Almeta, pp084-085
X2 Kui Buri, p097

**Jeremy Woodhouse,
Getty**
Bangkok city view,
inside front cover

BANGKOK
A COLOUR-CODED GUIDE TO THE HOT 'HOODS

CHATUCHAK
There's more to see here than the market, especially at night when this area comes alive

OLD TOWN
Where Chinatown met luxury hotel development and lost. The Chao Phraya is fascinating

SUKHUMVIT
Not so much a district as a traffic-clogged road. Pick your stopping points carefully

SIAM
A study of shopping contrasts: air-con malls to one side, neon-lit lanes to the other

SILOM AND SATHORN
Gay bars, lady-boy shows and destination dining all lie close to the city's financial heart

ROYAL CITY AVENUE
Open until late, this former student haunt has transformed itself into a nightlife hub

For a full description of each neighbourhood,
including the places you really must not miss, see the Introduction